All About Bears

Written by Tamara Lubic
and Barbara Peacock

Here is a **big** bear.

There is a **little** bear.

A baby bear is a **cub**.

Look at the
brown bear.

This fish is a
salmon.

Look at the white bear. It is a **polar bear**.

Polar bears live in the **Arctic**.

A polar bear likes to swim.

Look at the black and white bear. It is a **panda bear**.

Panda bears eat **bamboo**.

A panda bear likes to climb trees.

A bear has a big body and four legs.

Ear
Eye
Nose
Mouth
A bear can smell very well.

A bear can walk on two legs.

A bear can run fast.